make the change

Also by Julia Barnard

Promoting Happiness: a workbook to help you appreciate and get the most out of your life

50 Ways to Increase Your Happiness

How to be Happy: a collection of 60 happiness writings

Online Counselling: a therapist's guide

Vegetarian Tapas: 150 quick and delicious snacks and bites for sharing

make the change

Over 250 Tips for Your Wellbeing and Happiness

Julia Barnard

MTC BOOKS

MTC Books
PO Box 356
McLaren Vale
SA 5171
Australia
books@makethechange.com.au

National Library of Australia Cataloguing-in-Publication entry:
Barnard, Julia, author

Make the change : over 250 tips for your wellbeing and happiness / Julia Barnard.

ISBN: 9780980759068 (paperback)
Well-being.
Happiness.
Self-actualization (Psychology).
158.1

ISBN 978-0-9807590-6-8

Cover design by Pandelaide

http://makethechange.com.au

Introduction

Welcome to the paperback edition of Make the Change: over 250 tips for your wellbeing and happiness. In fact there are actually 255 tips. I've finally counted them. The book contains an assortment of tips, all geared towards giving you a positive boost. I offer ideas to help you appreciate your life, achieve your goals, have fun, build better relationships, develop your optimism, relax and so much more. There are opportunities for personal reflection and growth and you don't even need to visit a counsellor's office. You will find mood boosters, health tips and ideas for change. They all have a common goal: greater wellbeing and happiness.

These tips have been on a long journey. They began life as 'tip of the week' on my website http://makethechange.com.au and later in my accompanying newsletters. I then set them up as a Google gadget which people could publish on their websites and desktops. In 2010 I went on to compile a PDF where readers could access all the tips I had written. The kindle edition arrived in 2011. Now they are available for the first time in this paperback edition. This edition sees the return of the notes section which was removed for the kindle edition. Now you can keep track of your notes and ponderings as you read through the tips.

Hopefully this will encourage you to be an active participant in your happiness journey.

The tips are presented in no particular order. Start at the beginning or pick a page at random. You can read one a day, one a week or as the mood grabs you. It's your choice. I suggest that for each tip, take a moment to reflect on it and take notes if you like. You can also come back after applying the tip to your life and make a note of your thoughts.

You may want to consider:

- How the tip is relevant to you personally.
- How you might apply it in your life.
- How you have successfully applied it.
- Changes you have seen in yourself.
- Any changes seen in the people around you after you have applied the tip.
- Making a note when you come across a particular tip you would like to learn more about.

I hope you enjoy these tips and use them for a happier and healthier life.

Best wishes

Julia Barnard

Have a productive day

I wish you a good morning. Now turn your good morning into a good day. Spend a few minutes writing down the reasons why you should have a productive day. How will it benefit you? What about other people? What are the drawbacks of not being productive? Also, think about how you know you will feel after a productive day.

Notes:

_____

_____

_____

_____

_____

_____

_____

_____

Energy tips for a better day

Make sure you have enough energy to get the most out of that fantastic life of yours. Eat your breakfast – every day. Keep regular contact with a friend who never fails to inspire. Exercise regularly, making sure you find something that you enjoy doing. Of course, sleep well – you need it to restore those depleted energy levels and start over the next day.

Notes:

_____

_____

_____

_____

_____

_____

_____

Where you live

Given much thought lately to the town you live in? Whether you chose it or not, this place is your home. So take the time to reflect on what's good about it. Why do you like living there? What does it have to offer? If somebody was visiting – where would you tell them to go? One weekend you could even get out and about with your camera and take snaps of all the good things.

Notes:

_____

_____

_____

_____

_____

_____

_____

_____

Discover your creativity

Try to do something creative every day. You do not have to be a 'creative type' to be creative. Creativity can refer to a new way of doing things; it is not just about expressing yourself artistically. It can be about trying something new at home or at work, developing an existing hobby or branching out and learning something new.

Notes:

Set a goal a week

At the start of each week, set yourself a goal. Make it something that you can accomplish in that week. It can be something you want to change, to try, or to finally finish. You may want to increase or decrease certain behaviour. It can be just for fun. Whatever it is, begin by saying to yourself: "this week I will...." Then get on and do it.

Notes:

_____

_____

_____

_____

_____

_____

_____

_____

Have some perspective

When contemplating future events, try to accept that the worst does not always happen, so don't assume it will. If you are prone to such 'all or nothing' thinking try to challenge your automatic thoughts and ask yourself how likely that gloomy scenario you are contemplating is to happen.

Notes:

_____
_____
_____
_____
_____
_____
_____

Do a good deed for a friend

Carrying out good deeds for other people has a double benefit. Not only does it enhance the life of the person you have given to, but it also helps you feel good about yourself. Giving is a great way to boost happiness and who better to help than a friend?

Notes:

_____
_____
_____
_____
_____
_____
_____
_____

Honesty

Try to be honest with your thoughts and feelings.
Saying how you feel will boost your confidence as
you know you are being true to yourself. Also,
being honest is not about being rude. You do not
need to tread on other people's feelings to get
across your own.

Notes:

_____
_____
_____
_____
_____
_____
_____

Read a novel

A great way to unwind and escape from the stresses of the day is to read a novel. Devoting your energies to the characters and plot within the pages stops you fretting about your own concerns and is a great way to relieve boredom.

Notes:

_____

_____

_____

_____

_____

_____

_____

Know that you can be happy

Being responsible for your own happiness means you are also responsible for your own sadness. Sometimes you just want to dwell and feel blue. The powerful thing to realise is that you have the tools at your disposal to help you be happy again tomorrow. Try to recognise that your sadness is fleeting and life will be good again.

Notes:

_____

_____

_____

_____

_____

_____

_____

Revive your motivation

Sometimes your motivation needs a bit of a boost, whether it is in relation to your job, your relationship, goals, anything. Take time to think about why you started the task in the first place, why you do what you do. Perhaps consider the deeper meaning behind what you do. Then use practical steps to cultivate that meaning.

Notes:

_____

_____

_____

_____

_____

_____

_____

Don't give up

Practise your determination. Make yourself keep going, even when you don't want to. Keep trying and trying, noting what you are learning about yourself and others along the way. Maintain a belief of optimism that things will get better, or turn out okay. Make sure your thoughts are not self-defeating and ignore the cynicism of others.

Notes:

_____

_____

_____

_____

_____

_____

_____

Schedule a laughter weekend

What are you doing next Sunday afternoon? How about gathering your favourite comedy DVDs, shutting the curtains, sinking into your sofa and enjoying a few hours of laughter? For greater benefits, gather a few friends to enjoy the time together. Remember, laughter is good for you, so this time is not frivolous. It's therapy.

Notes:

_____

_____

_____

_____

_____

_____

_____

_____

Make your own choices

Imagine going out to dinner. Where are you going to go? What main will you have? Will you have a starter? What will you drink? How about dessert? Coffee? So many choices to make! In fact, in this situation it's easy to defer to others, letting them decide for you. "What are you having?" "Are you having dessert?" "I'll have what you're having." These are words you may easily find yourself saying. However, by exercising your power of choice, you will probably enjoy your meal so much more. So be brave — choose a starter, a main, your choice of tipple and a scrummy dessert (if you fancy it!).

Notes:

_____

_____

_____

_____

_____

_____

_____

Finding meaning in your day

When was the last time you did something meaningful? Think back to yesterday. Can you derive meaning and purpose from the tasks you did? They do not have to be life changing, just worth doing. Such reflections give you a chance to think about how well you used your day. Hopefully you will recognise that procrastination is not the way to a meaningful life.

Notes:

_____

_____

_____

_____

_____

_____

_____

_____

Know your distractions

Want to exert greater control over your daily routine and life in general? Then spend time identifying the things you know generally distract you from doing the task you really want to be doing. Write them down — this makes it real. Then, resolve to avoid these distractions whilst working on a particular project. It may help to allocate a specific time in your day to these distractions. As such, they become tasks in their own right and something to look forward to.

Notes:

_____

_____

_____

_____

_____

_____

_____

Choose your role models with care

If you want a life of health and happiness, take care in who you choose as your role model. Celebrities and their lives are constantly in the media and it is easy to latch on to a particular celebrity's lifestyle choice. Fad dieting and extreme regimes are not the way to good health and wellbeing however. I have yet to see research that says thin people are happiest. As such, seek out people who live healthy, balanced lifestyles. Of course, you may have to look further afield than Hollywood to do this.

Notes:

_____

_____

_____

_____

_____

_____

_____

_____

Your achievements

Starting today, keep a journal of your life's achievements. Small things, as well as the grander successes. Keep track of what's going on in the here and now, as well as leaving space to record achievements from your past. When you have a low moment, be sure to take out your journal and read through it, reminding yourself how great you really are.

Notes:

_____

_____

_____

_____

_____

_____

_____

That's just not me

Have you ever done something that is at odds with how you perceive yourself? Something that has challenged your beliefs about who you are and the sort of things you do. What I am talking about are the times when you have stepped outside of your comfort zone and gone on to exceed all expectations of yourself. Hopefully you recognise that what you did is in fact part of you. As such you will need to create a new, updated perception of self.

Notes:

_____

_____

_____

_____

_____

_____

_____

_____

Eat, drink, sleep

Having the right snack or drink before bed can help you get a better night's sleep. Try eating a slice of toast washed down with a warm glass of milk. Toast contains carbohydrates and together with the amino acids in the milk, increases serotonin. Serotonin becomes melatonin, which is the hormone that aids sleep.

Notes:

_____

_____

_____

_____

_____

_____

_____

Getting social flow

If you are unsure whether to spend your free time doing things alone or with others, recent research suggests doing things with others results in greater feelings of joy. Although any flow experience can increase happiness levels, people tend to feel even better when such experiences are carried out in the company of other people. So choose an activity that challenges you and go for it.

Notes:

_____

_____

_____

_____

_____

_____

_____

_____

Exercising and your health

Regular exercise offers many benefits to your physical health. It protects against injury, strengthens bones (which can help prevent osteoporosis) and helps reduce blood pressure. Furthermore, it can reduce the risk of stroke, cardiovascular disease and the development of some cancers. Exercise can also help prevent the onset of Type 2 diabetes.

Notes:

_____
_____
_____
_____
_____
_____
_____

Making changes

Is there anything you would like to change? Better time management? Improved public speaking? A healthier diet? Increased knowledge of World War One? Whatever it happens to be, try researching everything you can on the subject. Get books out of the library or go online. If you are going for a behavioural or emotional change, try to steer clear of books that promote a sense of victim and prohibit change. You want strategies for change, not the opportunity to wallow. Set yourself a plan, try out different strategies, take your time and be proud of your accomplishments.

Notes:

_____

_____

_____

_____

_____

_____

_____

Quick guide to a flow experience

If you want to be happy, one way is through a flow experience. You choose the activity, but it should be something that actively engages you (watching TV doesn't count). You will need to set a goal that is challenging enough for you to aspire to, but not so difficult it is nearly impossible to achieve. Finally, take steps to ensure you get regular feedback on your progress. Easy!

Notes:

_____

_____

_____

_____

_____

_____

_____

Exercise for good mental health

Engaging in regular exercise is important to your psychological health because it helps relieve symptoms of stress and anxiety, boosts mood and can help prevent depression. It's also a great way to achieve flow as it provides you with opportunities to work on goals and challenges. It can even improve body image and do wonders for your self-confidence.

Notes:

_____

_____

_____

_____

_____

_____

_____

_____

Ray of sunshine

Did you know that the quickest way to get your dose of Vitamin D is to go outside? To benefit you will need to go out without sunscreen; however, just five minutes will do. Vitamin D has been shown to boost mood, increase energy and aid sleep. A deficiency has been associated with depression.

Notes:

_____

_____

_____

_____

_____

_____

_____

Try a new ingredient

Varying what you eat not only keeps things interesting, it also helps you meet all your nutritional needs. When you next go shopping, keep an eye out for something you have never had before. If you're not sure how to cook it, search through your cookbooks or look on the web. Also, when in a restaurant, take the chance on eating something different. If you don't like it, you never have to eat it again.

Notes:

_____

_____

_____

_____

_____

_____

_____

_____

Small moments of happiness

Don't wait for a major event to bring you happiness. Instead note down the small things that bring you happiness. Then make an effort to carry them out on a regular basis. Small, everyday pleasures that you give yourself can have a great impact on your mood. It also means you always have something to look forward to.

Notes:

_____

_____

_____

_____

_____

_____

_____

A trip to the museum

Take a trip to a museum or art gallery. Find something that moves you and spend time reflecting on and appreciating its beauty. What good feelings does it bring out in you? Try to hold on to these feelings as you carry on with your day. If you cannot get to a museum, you could always search the internet for images of art depicting a subject that interests you.

Notes:

_____
_____
_____
_____
_____
_____
_____
_____

Admit your mistakes

When you make a mistake, what do you do? Do you own up to it, openly acknowledging what you have done, resolving to learn from your error? Or do you keep quiet, choosing to say nothing, instinctively hoping you won't be found out? Or do you choose to blame another person for your act, or let them take the fall? Owning up to your errors is the fair thing to do — both to yourself and other people.

Notes:

_____
_____
_____
_____
_____
_____
_____

Keep your promises

If you make a promise to someone, make an effort to keep it. Whether it's to your partner, your boss, your staff, friends or children. If you don't keep it, you'll be letting that person down and your word will no longer be trusted. Even if that person says nothing and you think it's okay — both of you know deep down that you have broken your word.

Notes:

_____

_____

_____

_____

_____

_____

_____

_____

Reasons to be happy

I always feel disappointed when I see people criticising the notion of happiness and positivity. It seems to promote a sense of hopelessness and an attitude of 'why bother'. So I suggest you come up with as many reasons as you can for why promoting happiness is a good thing. You could draw on your own experiences, or go one step further and discover the research out there that highlights the many benefits happiness brings to both your mental and physical wellbeing.

Notes:

_____

_____

_____

_____

_____

_____

_____

Your significant other

Spend some time thinking about all the things you love about your significant other. What characteristics do you like? In what ways do you admire them? Think about why you are glad they are in your life. If you feel inclined, you could even share some of your thoughts with them.

Notes:

_____

_____

_____

_____

_____

_____

_____

_____

Time for laughter

What makes you laugh? Try to think of as many different things as possible, including certain books, movies, comedians, websites and people you know. Now ask yourself: "when did I last have a good hearty chuckle?" Laughter brings with it many benefits. It lowers blood pressure, eases stress, may aid recovery from depression and may help reduce chronic pain.

Notes:

_____

_____

_____

_____

_____

_____

_____

Discover your family history

Do you know much about your family history? Learning about your ancestors and how they lived can be intriguing, exciting, gratifying and at the same time, a humbling experience. It is an opportunity to hear stories from your relatives as well as going back further in time. Chances are you will uncover a few surprises. Working back through history is an opportunity to increase gratitude for the life you have, as you reflect on the hardships of those gone before.

Notes:

_____

_____

_____

_____

_____

_____

_____

_____

Make time for your passion

What are you passionate about? What do you absolutely love and cannot wait to spend time doing? Well this week you need to make time for that passion — you will feel better for it. Not sure if you have a passion, or feel the word 'passion' is a bit strong? You could at least find time to do the things you enjoy and really engage in the moment. Want to find your passion? Then try something new. You could discover something that gives you a new found zest for life.

Notes:

_____

_____

_____

_____

_____

_____

_____

No more parental blame

You can blame your parents for many things: your terrible past, anxious present and the reason why your future is doomed to failure. I think the odds are high that your parents thought the same thing about their parents. If you can acknowledge your parents as human, prone to making their own mistakes but not being responsible for yours, there's a chance you can take control of your life. It would not hurt to think about the good qualities they brought to their parenting that helped nurture all the good qualities you have today.

Notes:

_____

_____

_____

_____

_____

_____

_____

_____

Compliments

Sometimes we can struggle with being totally honest both with ourselves and with others. However, an easy way to get started is to only compliment a person when you mean it. If your instinct is to say 'nice dress' without considering if you mean it, pause and ask yourself if that's how you really feel. If it's not — say nothing.

Notes:

_____
_____
_____
_____
_____
_____
_____
_____

Get inspired

Are you running out of inspiration? Do you find yourself procrastinating over a task? Then take a break for a few minutes. Pause, look around you and see what is going on. Is there anything you see that can offer you renewed motivation or inspiration? Perhaps it's the hard working colleague in the corner? Or the not-so hard working colleague who pushes you into action, because you don't want to be like them. Maybe you have an inspirational quote that now is the time to re-read. Just observe and let what you see fire you up.

Notes:

_____
_____
_____
_____
_____
_____
_____
_____

Your family

Take the time to reflect positively on your family members. Think about their strengths and qualities, admire their ability to overcome hardships faced and focus on the good bits in their relationship with you. For an extra happiness boost, feel grateful they are in your life and try to forgive any past conflicts or transgressions.

Notes:

_____

_____

_____

_____

_____

_____

_____

School days

Remember your school days? Best time of your life, right? Maybe. Maybe not. If not, it's easy to focus on what was wrong: teachers you disliked, lessons you struggled with, the kids that bullied. Earlier experiences do impact on your life today. However, how about taking the time to think about what was good about school — the things you did enjoy? It will help change your perspective and heal old wounds.

Notes:

_____

_____

_____

_____

_____

_____

_____

_____

Days of the week

It is all too easy to live just for the weekend. Each week counting down the days until Saturday, effectively wishing your life away. Yet each day has its merits. Go through each day and think about what's good about it. Why is that day so great, in its own right? You may like to write your thoughts down and keep adding to your list. You could also do this the night before, as a reminder of what you have to look forward to.

Notes:

_____

_____

_____

_____

_____

_____

_____

Censor your emails

You probably send out many emails on a daily basis. As part of work, to friends and family or to chase up something. When writing your email, try to remember your tone. It's easy to believe you can get away with being rude via email. As you type, imagine you are speaking to the person face to face and keep your tone polite. Think about how it feels when you receive a rude email. Also, if you ask for help via email and they give it, it never hurts to acknowledge that help with a quick thanks.

Notes:

_____

_____

_____

_____

_____

_____

_____

_____

Liking yourself

So. Do you like you? I mean really like you? All that you are: your strengths, weaknesses, the things you say and do, what you look like, how you spend your time, your beliefs and values? In other words, everything that is you. It is important to accept yourself and trust who you are. Don't let other people's attitudes undermine your confidence.

Notes:

_____

_____

_____

_____

_____

_____

_____

Refresh your interests

Started a new hobby lately? Hopefully you are already doing what you enjoy and are making time for it. However, keep an eye out for new things to try and give them a go. It is an opportunity to challenge and surprise yourself as well as learn new skills. Whatever you choose, make sure you do it because you want to and it suits your personality. You want to enjoy it, after all.

Notes:

_____

_____

_____

_____

_____

_____

_____

_____

Problem solving to ease stress

Sometimes our emotions can get in the way of seeing things clearly. We end up feeling stuck, stressed and quite powerless. However, learning to problem solve is a great way to consider issues causing us concern. In brief, you need to brainstorm potential practical solutions to your problem. Then for each potential solution, weigh up the pros and cons. From here you are able to make a choice, which you can then carry out. Although it works best on paper, with practice you can work through the process in your head.

Notes:

_____

_____

_____

_____

_____

_____

_____

Share your happiness learnings

Don't keep what you know about happiness to yourself. Instead, look for opportunities to share your knowledge with others. Think about happiness boosters as well as those things that will probably hinder happiness. How about those tips that you know work particularly well for you? Consider sharing with people who could do with a pick me up or are cynical about the idea of enjoying life. If you offer them enough ideas, you never know what might sink in.

Notes:

_____

_____

_____

_____

_____

_____

_____

_____

Interact with your TV

When you next sit down to watch a TV program, try tuning in to the emotions you experience whilst you are watching. Do certain events affect you at quite a deep level? What sort of things make you laugh? Who are the characters you feel empathy for? What about those you dislike? Afterwards, spend a moment reflecting on what you learnt about yourself based on your emotional responses to the program. Were there any surprises?

Notes:

_____

_____

_____

_____

_____

_____

_____

Let music work for you

Listening to music can benefit you both mentally and physically. However, you want to choose the right sort of music to get the most from it. Upbeat music boosts mood, whereas slow tempo music helps you sleep. Classical music in particular can reduce blood pressure and help not only reduce stress but prevent its onset. It is important you choose tracks you enjoy however, because research has found listening to music people disliked led to blood vessels contracting — which is associated with the development of blood clots.

Notes:

_____

_____

_____

_____

_____

_____

_____

_____

Make conscious food choices

Are you aware of the feelings that arise from what you eat? Do you like your food? Try to tune in each time you sit down to eat and ask yourself if you are enjoying it. Then afterwards, ask yourself how you are feeling. Food should be savoured and appreciated. If you don't like how certain foods leave you feeling, don't eat them. Next time, choose something else. Giving yourself variety not only keeps things interesting, exciting your taste buds and helping you feel good, but it also means you are getting different nutrients each time.

Notes:

_____

_____

_____

_____

_____

_____

_____

Get environmentally creative

Use your creative talents to make use of things you would normally throw away. Whether it is old envelopes or packaging, give them a new lease of life. It could be for a functional purpose or you could create a piece of artwork. Think about ways you can use leftover food to create whole new recipes. You never know what you might invent.

Notes:

_____

_____

_____

_____

_____

_____

_____

_____

What don't you know?

Make a list of all the things you still don't know about your favourite areas of interest. This is an opportunity to increase your expertise and become more curious. Choose areas that pique your interest and set about learning more about them. Visit websites, chat on forums or read books and magazines on the subject. You never know where this new direction in an existing interest will take you.

Notes:

_____

_____

_____

_____

_____

_____

_____

Take control of your health

Happiness is not just a mind-state; it's about your behaviour also. As such, it is worth doing what you can to keep your body healthy. Don't be put off by the health messages you hear — leaving you feeling preached to. Instead take heed and choose to adopt one piece of health advice each month. Also, rather than feeling like a passive recipient of different messages, actively seek out information so you know why exercise is good for you, why stress is bad and why certain foods are unhealthy.

Notes:

_____

_____

_____

_____

_____

_____

_____

_____

Face your challenge with optimism

What did you do when you were last confronted with a challenge? Did you face it head on, or did you get angry, frustrated, pass it on to someone else, or just give up, declaring yourself a failure? When you next have a challenge, hold on to the optimistic belief that you will get through it and achieve what it was you'd set out to. Ask yourself if you are giving up too easily. Also, ask for assistance if this will help you through the challenge.

Notes:

_____

_____

_____

_____

_____

_____

_____

_____

Sunrise / sunset

If you have a chance, get outside and appreciate a sunrise. Enjoy the moment as you relish in the colours and the dramatic changes it brings. Look forward to the day ahead. If you missed the sun rise, keep an eye out for sunset. Again, you will experience amazing beauty and its calming effect will give you the chance to reflect on your day. Take photos for a week and see just how varied each one is.

Notes:

_____

_____

_____

_____

_____

_____

_____

_____

Look at the weather

What's going on outdoors? Each season brings different changes, so take a moment to look out of your window and observe these. What's the weather doing? What colours are apparent? Are you noticing the appearance of different birds and animals? Try to appreciate each day and how it reflects the season you are in.

Notes:

_____

_____

_____

_____

_____

_____

_____

Forgiveness in others

If you struggle to forgive, take a moment to recall times when other people have forgiven you. They may not have said the words "I forgive you", but they were willing to reconcile and get past your actions. Remember how glad you were that they were able to forgive you and recognise how it would feel to another person if you were now to forgive them.

Notes:

_____
_____
_____
_____
_____
_____
_____
_____

Don't be in such a hurry

How about slowing down for a bit? Taking care over what you do can help you make fewer mistakes, get the task done right the first time and will essentially ease the pressure. This is particularly appropriate when driving. If you are the sort of driver that has to go faster than the speed limit or is constantly jumping lanes, take a moment to pause, relax, sit back and enjoy the journey. You'd have only got to your destination a few minutes earlier (provided you haven't had an accident). And let's be honest, what do you do with those precious minutes you were determined to gain?

Notes:

_____

_____

_____

_____

_____

_____

_____

Tune into your body clock

When are you at your best? Is it early morning or late at night? Do you really come to life after lunch, or is this time a struggle for you? Try to be aware of when you are at your best and use these times to get the most from your day. Although you may not be able to control when you go to work, it can give you a good idea of when to work on a particular project. It can also help you decide the best time to exercise.

Notes:

_____

_____

_____

_____

_____

_____

_____

_____

Look out for your team

A successful team is not one where members try to undermine the work or actions of another member, in order that they receive the most personal gain. Working together, supporting each other, listening to and respecting ideas are some of the keys to good teamwork. The next time you are in a team, give some thought to any changes you can make (whether within yourself, or for the team as a whole) that will bring your group in line with what constitutes a successful team.

Notes:

_____

_____

_____

_____

_____

_____

_____

_____

Don't steal

If you want to live a good, happy life, then presumably not stealing from other people should be an obvious way forward. However, it is not just about taking other people's material possessions. How about another person's ideas, thoughts or words? If somebody has an idea you like, give them full credit — don't just take it for your own. This is particularly relevant to the workplace. Have you ever sat in a meeting and a colleague suggests an idea as their own which you had suggested to them only yesterday? Don't be like that colleague.

Notes:

_____

_____

_____

_____

_____

_____

_____

_____

Dedication to the cause

Choose one goal. It should be one that is important to you. Now dedicate yourself to achieving this goal. Focus all your energies on the task, pulling out all the stops. Really commit yourself — nothing can stop you. Make time to work on it on a daily basis. Setbacks are merely challenges to be overcome, making the victory even greater. You may like to keep a record of your progress so you can see how far you have come.

Notes:

_____

_____

_____

_____

_____

_____

_____

Change your perception of work

Feeling uninspired and fed up at work, but are in no position to bring about change? If so, for one week, put on a pair of rose-tinted glasses and challenge your long-held negative perception of work. Focus on those parts of your working day that you find enjoyable. It's easy to overlook such elements as you become focused on the bad. Also, try to become aware of the people within your workplace who do good, bring pleasure and are motivational and funny. Ignore the miserables that you normally zoom in on. Keep practising and you may start feeling better about work and yourself.

Notes:

_____

_____

_____

_____

_____

_____

_____

_____

Your passion

For a happier life, it is generally suggested that people find their passion and pursue it. Could it be however, that you have already found your passion but you still find yourself searching for it? It was there, right under your nose. You just took it for granted because it's already part of who you are. Well if this is you, stop searching for something new and devote regular time to the passion that's already in your life. To keep things interesting, try taking it to the next level.

Notes:

_____
_____
_____
_____
_____
_____
_____

Honesty with others

How important is honesty to you? Are you as honest with others as you expect other people to be with you? Sometimes it's easy to demand that people be honest with us, but then we fail to live up to these expectations. Remember to be honest with yourself when answering this question. Now, who is the most honest person you know? How might you use them as a role model to increase your own sense of integrity?

Notes:

_____

_____

_____

_____

_____

_____

_____

_____

Be yourself

Integrity is about expressing outwardly the person you really are on the inside. So ask yourself: "would my partner recognise me if they were observing me at work?", "would my boss recognise me sat with my family at the dinner table?" Obviously we take on different roles as we go through life, but within each, it is important to be yourself.

Notes:

_____
_____
_____
_____
_____
_____
_____

Persist at new challenges

Try learning something new and keep going until you have perfected it. Else take the time to perfect something you think you are not very good at, but you know you could improve given time and patience. It could be something in relation to your hobbies, or your work or home routine. Know you can do it and you can do it well.

Notes:

_____

_____

_____

_____

_____

_____

_____

Happiness as a goal

Remember happiness has no end point. As such there is not one thing that will make you happy and that's it, you will be content forevermore. Happiness is ongoing. As such try to do things that increase your happiness on a day to day basis and enhance your sense of worth over time. Happiness is often the positive by-product of working towards meaningful goals.

Notes:

_____

_____

_____

_____

_____

_____

_____

Actions speak louder than words

Do your actions match what you say? Spend time monitoring your actions to see if they really do back up your words. It can give you a good insight into yourself as you can see how true to yourself you are being. What changes can you make to ensure one corresponds to the other? You can change what you say as well as what you do. Ideally your words and actions should reflect how you really think and feel.

Notes:

_____

_____

_____

_____

_____

_____

_____

Re-energise your routine

To increase your zest for life, give your routine a makeover. Think up ways you can inject more energy into your day. When you would normally slump in your chair, sit upright. Be alert to your surroundings rather than switching off and going into zombie-mode. Sing while you cook, make up games on the bus, go for a walk at lunchtime. Anything to mix things up and boost those energy levels. Remember to exercise regularly, eat right and sleep well.

Notes:

_____

_____

_____

_____

_____

_____

_____

Dealing with old arguments

Do you ever have the same argument over and over, whether with your partner or your children, and there's no apparent resolution? Try to take the time to step into their shoes. Think of at least three reasons why their opinion may be valid. You do not have to agree with them, but it may help you to become more open to their point of view. Remember, everyone is entitled to an opinion, even if it is different to yours.

Notes:

_____

_____

_____

_____

_____

_____

_____

_____

Significant moments

Take time to think about and write down the significant moments in your life. What have you done to make your life what it is today? It does not have to be a whole list of events. One or two meaningful moments are fine and probably quite realistic. Reflecting on these moments will help you realise how much control you do have in shaping your life.

Notes:

_____

_____

_____

_____

_____

_____

_____

Develop happy habits

You can learn to be happy. By taking just small steps you can develop new habits that are good for your health and wellbeing. Be the first to make up after an argument, sing in the shower, help out a friend, do some exercise. There are many possibilities. Carried out often enough, your new behaviours will become a way of life.

Notes:

_____

_____

_____

_____

_____

_____

_____

Challenge yourself

This week think about how you can challenge yourself; then do it! It may be varying your normal routine, learning something new or completing a task you have been avoiding. By stepping out of your comfort zone you give yourself an opportunity to develop as a person. Even if you are not happy with the outcome, at least you gave it a try and learnt something about yourself.

Notes:

_____

_____

_____

_____

_____

_____

_____

Change a habit

This week think about whether you are stuck in a rut. Is there a habit that you have had for years but no longer really works for you? It could be always eating a certain meal on Mondays, or using the same brand of soap. Whatever it is, whether large or small, think about making the change. Remind yourself that you are in charge and it was you that formed the habit in the first place.

Notes:

_____

_____

_____

_____

_____

_____

_____

_____

Other viewpoints

How open minded are you? Are you open to other opinions or do you firmly believe that there is only one right point of view and that's your own? This week, select a number of topics you have strong opinions on. Then think about and write down views and opinions that are opposite to yours. Try to see the other person's perspective. This is not about changing your opinion; it is about enhancing your awareness of the world and may help you be more open minded in the process.

Notes:

_____
_____
_____
_____
_____
_____
_____

Question your happy activities

What makes you happy? Write a list of the things you do regularly that bring you happiness. Now look at this list again. Ask yourself — does it really bring you happiness? How do you truly feel after you've carried out your chosen activity? Activities to be wary of include watching television, shopping, drinking alcohol, smoking and eating. What you think may bring you happiness may not do anything for your mood after all.

Notes:

_____

_____

_____

_____

_____

_____

_____

_____

No more fibs

Try to keep an eye on all the lies you tell. Even those small ones that you come out with, because you think it is for the benefit of another person. Bringing your lies into awareness enables you to realise how frequently you engage in such behaviours. Your next task is to try and reduce the amount of lies you tell each day, until you find yourself being open and honest at all times. Remember honesty is not the same as being rude or tactless.

Notes:

_____

_____

_____

_____

_____

_____

_____

Be prudent

When making a decision about something, try to consider the consequences of a particular choice further down the track. How will it impact you an hour, a day, even a year from now? Will the decision undermine your values or long term goals in any way? Such reflection can be used for the smaller decisions (will I regret that chocolate bar in an hour?), as well as more important decisions (shall I go for promotion or stay where I am?) in your life.

Notes:

_____

_____

_____

_____

_____

_____

_____

_____

Time to reflect

Remember when you were really happy? Remember that fun thing you did last year? Remember last weekend when you got to do exactly what you pleased? Reminiscing over happy past events can boost positive emotion. Recall how good you felt at the time, savour the experience and relive the moment. You can share your experiences with those that were there as well as those that were not, or just allow yourself a private recollection.

Notes:

_____

_____

_____

_____

_____

_____

_____

Enjoy your pleasures, but in moderation

What's your pleasure? Is it certain foods? Music? A particular film? To get the most satisfaction from your pleasures try not to indulge in them all the time. This is because you may start to take them for granted and get used to them; as such they are no longer a pleasure. Have them as something to look forward to: an occasional treat. Then when you're indulging, really enjoy the moment and make sure it is quality time.

Notes:

_____

_____

_____

_____

_____

_____

_____

_____

Make quick decisions

Can't decide where to go on holiday, which top to buy, or what film to see? There are so many choices today, that it can be overwhelming. In fact research has found that the more time you spend ruminating over possibilities, the unhappier you will be, once you decide. Probably because there may be a greater feeling of regret as you look at the choices you could have made. So try to reduce your choices (either limit the number of possibilities you will look at, or the time spent choosing) and make quicker decisions. Once decided, stick to it.

Notes:

_____
_____
_____
_____
_____
_____
_____

Past happy days

What sort of things have you engaged in over the years that have made you happy but you are no longer doing? Take your time to think about different activities you took part in. It may have been in your recent past or something you did years ago, possibly even as a child. Now look at your list. What can you start doing again? Commitments and lifestyle changes may mean the task takes on a different slant. The trick is to tailor the activity or activities (why stick at one?) to meet your present circumstances. Decide when and where and make it part of your routine.

Notes:

_____

_____

_____

_____

_____

_____

_____

_____

Listen to your favourite music

Find time this week to put on your favourite music. The great thing about listening to music is you can do other things at the same time, so even you busy people can make time for this. Of course, for maximum pleasure, sit back, relax and indulge in the pleasant feelings the music brings you.

Notes:

_____

_____

_____

_____

_____

_____

_____

What do you enjoy?

Think about all the things that you enjoy doing. Brainstorm as many things as possible, writing them down as you go. Now take the time to start integrating them into your daily life. Some may be easier to do than others, but just think, the more you do, the more pleasure you will have and hopefully the happier you will be.

Notes:

_____

_____

_____

_____

_____

_____

_____

_____

Go for a run

Running is a great way to increase your mood. Through running, endorphins are released into your body, giving you a natural high. Remember, any exercise will put you in a more positive mood; however running will leave you feeling great afterwards.

Notes:
_____
_____
_____
_____
_____
_____
_____
_____

Have a debate

One way to understand your feelings of fairness is to engage in an ethical debate. The thing about ethical debates is there is no right or wrong. Rather it is an expression of an opinion based on personal values. You may like to search the web for 'ethical dilemmas' and then take a stance. If you want to, you can then argue an opposing viewpoint. This will not only help you explore what is fair but will increase your open mindedness.

Notes:

_____

_____

_____

_____

_____

_____

_____

_____

Is that fair?

As you read a news article, particularly one outlining the outcome of a trial, ask yourself: is that fair? Fair to whom? All participants involved? The world at large? How about your own comfort zone? Such an activity can enhance your own understanding of what fairness means to you.

Notes:

_____

_____

_____

_____

_____

_____

_____

Get ahead

Want to feel in control of your day? Want to boost your efficiency and feelings of confidence? This week, try to meet a deadline ahead of time. It does not have to be a deadline given to you by others — it can be a self-imposed deadline. Even if you only finish a day or even hours earlier than scheduled, you will feel you have accomplished something. If you manage it, give yourself a reward for your effort.

Notes:

_____
_____
_____
_____
_____
_____
_____
_____

Keeping motivated

Each time you work on your goal, try to end when you are still feeling happy and motivated. Make a note of what you are doing and what you intend to do next. The next time you come back to your goal you will remember the good feelings associated with it and be in a nice position to pick up from where you left off.

Notes:

_____

_____

_____

_____

_____

_____

_____

Count your blessings

Each night, or each week, take a moment to reflect on the things you are grateful for in your life. Sometimes life can be a real struggle and it is hard to see the good. However, engaging in this task regularly will serve as a reminder of all the things that you are blessed with. It will help provide you with hope and a realisation that your life is not all bad. Try to think of personal aspects, as well as your environment and the people in your life.

Notes:

_____

_____

_____

_____

_____

_____

_____

_____

Forgive and be happy

If you want to be truly happy, try forgiving. You do not have to do it face to face. Forgiveness is for your benefit — write it in a diary, or tell a friend that you have forgiven the other person. You may have held a grudge against someone who has wronged you in the past and thinking about it still makes you unhappy. Being able to forgive enables you to move on in your life and embrace happier emotions. For future wrongs, try to forgive quickly so it does not get out of control and become a battle to overcome.

Notes:

_____

_____

_____

_____

_____

_____

_____

Cut down on passive activities

One way to increase your happiness levels is to reduce the amount of passive activities you engage in. The main culprit here is watching television. Instead involve yourself in activities that you can become absorbed in. Read a book, carry out a sport, cooking, gardening, your hobby. Enjoy it today and make it something to look forward to rather than the next episode of some program that in reality makes no difference to the quality of your life or your happiness.

Notes:

_____

_____

_____

_____

_____

_____

_____

_____

Develop your fairness strength

Fairness is a personal strength which can be nurtured and used in everyday life. One way you can use this strength is when the opportunity arises, make sure everybody has a turn. It could be an opportunity found in your home life, whether with your partner, friends, family or your children, as well as at work. It can be particularly relevant to those who manage people.

Notes:

_____

_____

_____

_____

_____

_____

_____

Setting goals

This week, write down all of your goals. Give yourself dates for when you intend to meet these goals. Also, write down exactly how you are going to achieve them. Break them down into small steps, and tick these off as you meet them. You could also think about a back-up plan if there are barriers to a particular goal which will prevent you from meeting it in the way you had desired.

Notes:

_____

_____

_____

_____

_____

_____

_____

_____

Look at the sky

To help put things into perspective, take time to look at the sky on a clear night. Gaze at the moon and the stars and wonder at the vastness of the universe. Suddenly all those little things you've been worrying about will hopefully not seem so bad.

Notes:

_____

_____

_____

_____

_____

_____

_____

Let go of the past

This week take time to reflect on yourself. Are you stuck in the past? It is easy to hold on to a time that you associate with better days. You may dress in 1970s gear, your house consists of 1970s decor and you may even act like you did back then. It's okay to move on and develop new hopes, dreams and a new you. Try to become the present — it's the best place to be.

Notes:

_____

_____

_____

_____

_____

_____

_____

_____

Set varied goals for the week

At the start of each week set yourself goals of things you would like to do. These should be achievable but varied. Carrying out such activities gives you focus and increases your happiness. Support for such intentional activity comes from research conducted by Lyubomirsky, Sheldon and David Schkade.

Notes:

_____

_____

_____

_____

_____

_____

_____

What you love about your life

Life is full of stress and sometimes it is easy to forget about the good things in your life. So this week take the time to list all those things that you love about your life as it is today. Think about who you are, what you do, your family, your friends, your environment. Everything that is you. Write down details. Why do you love the things you do? You can keep the list to refer to when things are getting you down.

Notes:

_____

_____

_____

_____

_____

_____

_____

_____

Time to have fun

Get in touch with your playful side. Life does not always have to be so serious. Try to make regular time to read the funnies in the newspaper, find an amusing website that makes you laugh or watch your favourite comedy show. Have a look for a quote that makes you laugh and display it somewhere where you can read it on a regular basis. It is possible to see the lighter side of all situations. Not only will you feel better, but you will be a pleasure to be around.

Notes:

_____

_____

_____

_____

_____

_____

_____

Laugh at yourself

This week, make an effort to lighten up. Take the opportunity to laugh at yourself. Try not to take yourself too seriously and if you make a mistake don't get defensive — laugh instead. Hopefully you will realise that what seemed so very dreadful, wasn't so bad after all.

Notes:

_____

_____

_____

_____

_____

_____

_____

_____

Support for learning

Want to learn more about a particular topic but lack the motivation? Engage in support groups that will boost your energies. Maybe take a class, join an online discussion group, or talk to friends or colleagues you know are also interested in the subject. Other people can be powerful motivators and inspire you into action.

Notes:

_____

_____

_____

_____

_____

_____

_____

Go on a date with your partner

Take the time to relive the early days of your relationship. Do this by going on a date similar to one you did when you first met. Spend time recalling how you got together, what attracted you to each other and generally relive those happy moments.

Notes:

_____
_____
_____
_____
_____
_____
_____
_____

Positive changes

Ask yourself, what positive change have you made to someone's life today? It doesn't have to be huge to make a difference. However, you should not underestimate the impact your positive actions may have made on their life. Such deeds will also help you feel better about yourself.

Notes:

_____

_____

_____

_____

_____

_____

_____

Diary of good things

Get yourself a diary or notebook. In here you can only put good things that you have experienced, or happy thoughts and feelings. Do it each day, adding things from your past, your present and things you are looking forward to. It can contain anything you want so long as it is the good stuff. Give it a name and be as arrogant as you like, for example, "John's Ego Book", "Full of Myself", "Me Me Me"!

Notes:

_____

_____

_____

_____

_____

_____

_____

_____

The qualities of others

Try to appreciate others in your group for the qualities they bring. The group may be your family, friends or work colleagues. It is easy to admire qualities that we strive for or are important to us. However, by raising your awareness of other strengths, it can lead to greater understanding, feelings of respect and better teamwork.

Notes:

_____

_____

_____

_____

_____

_____

_____

Thinking positive keeps you healthy

Having a positive outlook can serve you well at any stage in your life. It seems as an older person, if you stay positive about your developing frailty, the onset of that frailty is reduced. So keep positive, blitz the negative and go out and enjoy life.

Notes:

_____

_____

_____

_____

_____

_____

_____

Don't overgeneralise

If you want more harmony in your relationship, try not to overdramatise when your partner does something you disapprove of. Try to avoid the use of 'always'. Just because they made the mistake once, does not mean they always do it. Try to look for times when they don't carry out that despairing behaviour and acknowledge it when you see them doing it.

Notes:

_____

_____

_____

_____

_____

_____

_____

Never too old to learn

No matter how old you are, it is never too late to learn. So this week take time to learn something new. You don't have to enrol on a course (although you can if you wish), it could be something as simple as following up on that news article you read in the paper last week. It's so easy to stop learning once you leave school, but whether you are 25 or 75, you can still continue to increase your knowledge.

Notes:

_____

_____

_____

_____

_____

_____

_____

_____

Get a new perspective on an old issue

We all have regrets or bad times in our life. Sometimes we use them to justify being unhappy today. This exercise will hopefully help you realise that particular time in your life was not all negative. Take a large sheet of paper. In very small writing in the bottom right corner write out that unhappy event. Then use the rest of the paper to write out all the good things that happened during that time. Take as long as you like and try to fill the page.

Notes:

_____

_____

_____

_____

_____

_____

_____

_____

Love yourself

Stop worrying about what other people think. Instead invest your energy in loving yourself, accepting yourself and being proud and confident in all you do. There are no 'rules', so ignore any that people try to impose on you.

Notes:

_____

_____

_____

_____

_____

_____

_____

_____

Reflect on your values

What are your values? What is important to the way you run your life and how you regard other people? Do they still sit comfortably with the person you are today? Don't be afraid to reflect on and revise your values. Life and learning can change things, and what may have worked for you ten years ago may not sit so well with you now.

Notes:

_____
_____
_____
_____
_____
_____
_____
_____

Keep learning

So you want to become wiser? Then keep learning. Always. Throughout your life there will always be something new to learn. Take advice and receive support from others. You may learn something from the most unlikely places or people. By accepting that you are not all-knowing, you will be more curious and open-minded.

Notes:

_____

_____

_____

_____

_____

_____

_____

_____

Keep things in perspective

Harsh as this may sound, try to remember it's not all about you. In other words, as you go through your day, try to remember that everybody has their own set of issues, concerns, hopes and dreams. Their actions may have nothing to do with you at all. You can release yourself from a lot of anguish by taking this viewpoint, as you are not creating worries for yourself unnecessarily.

Notes:

_____

_____

_____

_____

_____

_____

_____

Accept yourself

Is it not time for you to accept yourself, warts and all? If only I was taller, smaller, cleverer, funnier... the list could go on. Instead turn these statements into positive statements. What's good about being small or tall? What are you good at? Why should you be funny? Of course, if there is something that you cannot accept about yourself and it is within your power to change, then do it!

Notes:

_____

_____

_____

_____

_____

_____

_____

_____

From negative to positive

Get hold of a blank notebook — this is your negatives to positives book. On the outside edge of the page write down the negative thought you have had for that day. Then on the rest of the page, challenge that thought, writing down as many positive statements as possible. Finally, rip the negative statement out of the book and throw it away. You are left with a book full of positives.

Notes:

_____

_____

_____

_____

_____

_____

_____

Read autobiographies

Spend time reading the autobiographies of people you admire. What inspiration do such people have to offer you? As you read, consider their unique insight into the world. What can you relate to? Reflect on the positive things you can take from their words.

Notes:

_____

_____

_____

_____

_____

_____

_____

_____

Discuss your day

Make time each day to discuss with your partner how your day has been. Take the time to listen to the other and then tell them what has been going on in your day. When doing this, try to note the good things going on in your partner's life. It also gives you an opportunity to reflect on your own day and note the positive things that have happened. You can also do this with your children.

Notes:

_____

_____

_____

_____

_____

_____

_____

Go for your goal

Have you a long-held goal that you never quite got around to completing? Do you believe you lack the courage to achieve it? Well take a look at that goal. Work out a plan of action for everything you need to do to reach that goal. Then break down your list into achievable chunks, giving yourself deadlines. Ask for help if needed. Then go for it. The pride you will feel will far outweigh the feelings of fear and anxiety that plagued you for so long. You will wonder what all the fuss was about.

Notes:

_____

_____

_____

_____

_____

_____

_____

_____

Stand up for your beliefs

Have you ever been in a situation where people were expressing opinions that differed to yours? What did you do next? Say something or keep quiet? Having the courage to speak up and express yourself shows your integrity. People may not agree with you and may not want to hear it but at least you are being true to yourself and the ideals you value so much.

Notes:

_____

_____

_____

_____

_____

_____

_____

Positive people

Try to surround yourself with positive people. Their energy and enthusiasm for life will soon rub off on you. Whereas, negative, miserable people will soon sap you of energy and you may come to see the world as they do. Although it may be difficult to avoid such people, do what you can to minimise the encounters and don't get drawn into their way of thinking.

Notes:

_____

_____

_____

_____

_____

_____

_____

_____

Resolutions

Do you like making resolutions for the New Year? The New Year can be an opportunity to start over, make the changes you want in your life or break habits you are finally sick of. However, you don't just have to wait for the New Year to start afresh. It can be anytime: the start of a new month, week or day. You could even resolve to change during the course of a day. Perhaps irritated by your endless procrastination, you resolve to never do it again, then get down to business straight after lunch. There's always an opportunity to start over and be inspired.

Notes:

_____

_____

_____

_____

_____

_____

_____

Savour the flavour

This Christmas, rather than stuffing yourself full of food and then feeling guilty afterwards, try to enjoy everything you eat. Savour the different foods you eat, appreciating the taste and texture. Christmas time is the perfect opportunity to eat foods you do not generally have throughout the year, so you may as well appreciate them. If you are cooking, use different spices to add depth to your dishes and perhaps try cooking something new. And remember, making time to exercise will help prevent the holiday bulge and feelings of guilt. It will also reduce stress and lift your mood.

Notes:

_____
_____
_____
_____
_____
_____
_____
_____

Find like-minded people

The great thing about the Internet is it allows you to connect with people all over the world who have interests similar to yours. You can also find people who can offer a great deal of support when you need it, especially during difficult times when you can believe that you are the only one experiencing certain things. So if you are trying to renew an interest in a hobby or want to feel less alone, seek out discussion forums and websites that can assist.

Notes:

_____

_____

_____

_____

_____

_____

_____

Be kind to yourself

Are you working on a goal that's important to you? Perhaps you are learning something new and can't wait to be an expert. Try to reign in this sense of urgency to get to the end. Instead, be kind and allow yourself to enjoy the journey. Take one step at a time and don't be afraid to go back and review what you have learned. If you are feeling stuck or frustrated, perhaps you might seek out the support of others to help you through it.

Notes:

_____

_____

_____

_____

_____

_____

_____

_____

Think positive

Spend this week being positive. If negative thoughts creep in, stop them and turn them into a positive. The more you do it, the more it will become a habit and a part of who you are.

Notes:

_____

_____

_____

_____

_____

_____

_____

Read your favourite novel

Feeling fed up? Need time out, to get away from the stresses of your day? Then grab a favourite novel, choose your favourite place to sit, then get stuck in. Books are a great way to escape and reading a book that you love, or an author that you can rely upon to meet your needs, can be the perfect way to unwind. The great thing about reading is you can do it for as long as you like. So if you only have ten minutes, fine. An hour, even better.

Notes:

_____

_____

_____

_____

_____

_____

_____

_____

Sleep well

If you want to be happy, full of life and have the energy to pursue your goals, you will want to make time for sleep. Sleep is important for our wellbeing and not enough can affect both our physical and mental health. Try to get eight hours of sleep each night. If you have problems sleeping, try turning the TV off earlier, skip the coffee and do something that relaxes you just before you go to bed.

Notes:

_____

_____

_____

_____

_____

_____

_____

Your purpose in life

So, have you worked out the purpose of your life yet? This is not an easy thing to answer, so allow time to explore and reflect. Remember, this is something personal to you and never has to be shared with others. Once you have your answer, how might you live your life so you are able to fulfil that purpose? What practical things can you do on a daily basis that will allow you to achieve this momentous goal?

Notes:

_____
_____
_____
_____
_____
_____
_____
_____

Brag less

If you want to increase your modesty, try to note how often you boast about the things you do. Do you show off your talents and achievements, especially around people you deem to be inferior to you in some way? Having noticed how you behave, take steps to cut down how often you do it. Instead, let your actions speak for you.

Notes:

_____
_____
_____
_____
_____
_____
_____

Look to your past

If you are facing a current dilemma or difficulty in your life, try using your past experience for inspiration. Recall difficulties in your past. What did you do to overcome them? Who did you turn to for support? Is there anything that experience tells you works better than other possibilities? Your past concern does not have to be the same as what you are facing presently to be of use to you. As you resolve your present dilemma, make a mental note of what worked for you so you can draw on this in the future.

Notes:

_____

_____

_____

_____

_____

_____

_____

_____

The happiest person

If you were the happiest person in the world, what would you be doing? How would you spend your days? Who would you spend them with? Now is there any chance of making this a reality (at least for some of the time)?

Notes:

_____

_____

_____

_____

_____

_____

_____

Listen more, talk less

Monitor yourself the next time you are with a group of people. Do you find yourself being the loudest, informing the group of how great you are, barely listening to others? If you want to increase your humility, try to spend more time listening to others, avoiding the temptation to tell people about your own achievements or trying to bring the conversation back to you. Notice how it feels to do this and reflect on the change it brings.

Notes:

_____
_____
_____
_____
_____
_____
_____
_____

Support others

Do you know someone who is trying to change a particular behaviour or develop new habits? For example, your partner is trying to stop unhealthy snacking. Make the effort to support them in their mission and help them uphold their plan when times get difficult. Friends and family can unwittingly sabotage their loved one's plans, allowing them to break their rules, rather than questioning their actions. So instead, remind them of their goal and how they will regret their behaviour.

Notes:

_____

_____

_____

_____

_____

_____

_____

Optimists persist

When faced with a challenge, don't give up. If you are wondering if your efforts are wasted, look at the situation objectively and ask yourself what you can do to enhance your chances of success. An optimist will keep trying, work hard and as such, will be more likely to succeed. They do not assume they are doomed to fail as soon as they hit an obstacle. So be persistent and be patient.

Notes:

_____

_____

_____

_____

_____

_____

_____

_____

What's so special about you?

It's time to acknowledge how unique you are. Think about the qualities, characteristics, experiences, skills and talents that when put together make up you. Now consider how you are going to use this uniqueness in your life. How can it help you reach your goals? How can it make the world a better place? How can it make life more enjoyable?

Notes:

_____

_____

_____

_____

_____

_____

_____

_____

Write out your regrets

How's your self-control? Do you sometimes do something that you know violates your goals and standards or undermines how you feel about yourself? For example, eating too many donuts then ALWAYS regretting it afterwards. To help gain control, write down exactly why this behaviour is a mistake, preferably at the moment you experience the regret. Then put this piece of paper somewhere where you can remind yourself how you will feel when you start to get tempted once more.

Notes:

_____
_____
_____
_____
_____
_____
_____
_____

Deep breathing

This week have a go at deep breathing. Inhale slowly and calmly through your nose, filling your lungs. As you do so imagine breathing in the positive. Then exhale slowly out through your mouth and as you do so, release all the negative. Such an exercise will help calm your thoughts and hopefully leave you feeling more relaxed.

Notes:

_____

_____

_____

_____

_____

_____

_____

Resist temptation

This week, work to deliberately resist a particular temptation and reward yourself positively for your discipline. Such temptations can be particular foods, alcohol, swearing, watching TV or surfing the web when you should be doing something else. Whatever it is that is getting in the way of you achieving your goal. Make sure your reward is not indulging in the temptation you so successfully resisted.

Notes:

_____
_____
_____
_____
_____
_____
_____
_____

Ten people who have influenced your life

Write a list of ten people who have had an influence on the life you have today. They do not necessarily have to be people you know, simply people you admire. Then think about how they made a difference. Don't forget, keep it positive!

Notes:

_____

_____

_____

_____

_____

_____

_____

Keep a secret

If someone tells you something in confidence, keep it to yourself. It is easy to believe that spreading gossip will make you friends as you are the one 'in the know'. However, people will learn not to trust you as they will come to notice what you do with the information. If you struggle to keep a secret, imagine how you would feel if something you confided to another was around the office within an hour.

Notes:

_____

_____

_____

_____

_____

_____

_____

_____

Think optimistically

When bad things happen to optimists, they don't expect it to last. Start training your brain so that when stressful, difficult situations come up, you tell yourself that you will get through it and that the situation will not last. Is there anything practical you can do to help you through the situation sooner? This technique can apply to small things like waiting for a delayed train (realise it will come eventually, rather than it's never going to arrive) as well as large events such as messing up an important job interview (know you can do better and resolve to learn from what went wrong previously).

Notes:

_____
_____
_____
_____
_____
_____
_____
_____

Listen to someone

The next time you're having a chat with someone, really listen to what they have to say. Don't use it as an opportunity to have your say. Don't jump in, talk over them or finish their sentences. Take your time and you'll probably learn something about that person, as well as yourself. Leave the conversation feeling good about yourself. Chances are the other person will feel happy as well.

Notes:

_____
_____
_____
_____
_____
_____
_____
_____

Make time for your friends

This week, find the time to meet up with your friends. If you are unable to do this, at least give them a call or send them a letter, email or a card, so they know you are thinking of them. Friendships are important to our wellbeing and have been found to be influential in reducing stress.

Notes:

_____

_____

_____

_____

_____

_____

_____

Learn something new

To maintain happiness, it is important to keep your life from becoming too routine. One way to do this is to learn something new. It gives you a new focus, absorbs your energy and exercises those brain cells! It can be anything, so long as you have never tried it before. Learn an instrument, take up a language, learn how to touch type, juggle, or use chopsticks. If you don't like it, try something else! Have fun.

Notes:

_____

_____

_____

_____

_____

_____

_____

_____

Share your positive thoughts

Think of three good things you would say about your partner, friend or family member. Think about their positive actions, strengths and displays of character. Having compiled your three good things, share them with that person. Not only will you feel good for sharing, but you will boost their happiness also.

Notes:

_____

_____

_____

_____

_____

_____

_____

Listen to others

If you want to be a great leader, it is important for you to listen to the ideas of others. Your team will appreciate you for it and it will help gain their respect. A good leader values and respects the opinions of others and is not too arrogant to believe that they always know best.

Notes:

_____
_____
_____
_____
_____
_____
_____
_____

Give yourself a regular flow experience

What is a flow experience? It is a concept coined by Csikszentmihalyi to describe those moments when you are so absorbed in an activity that everything else is forgotten, even the time. You get that feel-good buzz afterwards from having engaged in something engrossing. So try to find activities in your life that enable a regular flow experience. Engage regularly and you will feel much happier.

Notes:

_____

_____

_____

_____

_____

_____

_____

Support

Don't be afraid to ask for support when it is needed. Your friends, family and colleagues can assist you in many ways, from practical help, offering an opinion, giving encouragement or just being there to listen. Also, if someone offers to help you, don't automatically knock them back. There is no rule that says you should always go it alone.

Notes:

_____

_____

_____

_____

_____

_____

_____

_____

Am I happy?

This week ask yourself, "am I happy?" Write down all the things you are happy about and all the things you are unhappy about. Look at your unhappy list. What can you change? What steps can you take to reduce your unhappy list? It may be there are some things that you cannot change as they are out of your control. If so, what steps can you take to accept these things so you can feel more positive about them?

Notes:

_____
_____
_____
_____
_____
_____
_____

Engage in the present

One moment this week, stop what you are doing and engage in the present. What are you doing? How are you feeling? What can you see, hear, smell, taste and touch? Forget about the past and don't worry about the future. Just enjoy the here and now.

Notes:

_____
_____
_____
_____
_____
_____
_____
_____

Positive talk

Never, ever, say "I can't." If you start to talk negatively to yourself, you will come to believe it. So keep all your talk positive. You can do it. If those negative thoughts creep in shout "stop". There's no room in your mind for thoughts like that.

Notes:

_____

_____

_____

_____

_____

_____

_____

Become an expert

Do you want to be good at something? How about really good? Then you need to practise. Any skill takes work. To assist you, try to get feedback and support from other people on a regular basis. Also, try to conduct frequent self-evaluations so you can think about how you can improve. It is all very well practising the same thing over and over (that song you really like playing on the guitar), but to become an expert you will need to step out of your comfort zone and tackle the trickier things. Remember to enjoy yourself along the way, of course.

Notes:

_____

_____

_____

_____

_____

_____

_____

_____

Stop multitasking

When we multitask, we are constantly thinking ahead and are unable to give 100% commitment to a single task. To increase pleasure in your day, try focusing on one task at a time. Carry it out with purpose and dedication. You will find increased satisfaction in all you do — and that includes the small things. It may even help reduce stress.

Notes:

_____

_____

_____

_____

_____

_____

_____

Defend a friend

If you find yourself amongst a group of people who are being critical of one of your friends, don't join in. Even better, have courage and come to your friend's defence. It's sometimes easier to follow the majority opinion, even if you don't believe it. Would you not want your friend to do the same if they were in your place?

Notes:

_____

_____

_____

_____

_____

_____

_____

_____

Question your unhelpful beliefs

The way we think can have a profound impact on our wellbeing. Holding on to negative beliefs is always unhelpful. Believing we are not good enough, not worthy, fearing failure and being racked with guilt all contribute to unhappiness. It is important to challenge these beliefs. Are they true? Do they make sense? Where is the evidence? Once challenged, replace them with more realistic beliefs.

Notes:

_____
_____
_____
_____
_____
_____
_____

Keep an eye on your goal

If you have set yourself a goal, keep your focus. It is very easy to get distracted, since let's face it, life is full of distractions. Remind yourself as frequently as possible of your goal, so it never gets forgotten. Paint it on a giant sheet of paper if you have to!

Notes:

_____

_____

_____

_____

_____

_____

_____

_____

Buy someone a present

This week, buy someone a small gift that they are not expecting. Take pleasure in planning what to buy, buying the present, planning to give the present and then relish in the feeling of giving someone you love the chosen gift.

Notes:

_____

_____

_____

_____

_____

_____

_____

Try imagery

Imagery can be a powerful tool in helping you achieve your goals. If you find yourself struggling to achieve a task, imagine yourself carrying out the task with energy and enthusiasm. Visualise yourself reaching your goal. Ideally you should shut your eyes to help you. Once you stop the imagery, try again at finishing the task. Hopefully it will be easier for you and you may even enjoy it.

Notes:

_____

_____

_____

_____

_____

_____

_____

_____

Volunteer

Giving some of your time each week to help others is a great way to boost happiness. It does not have to take up much of your time, although the more you volunteer, the happier you will be. Get involved in an activity that you are interested in or maybe work with a group you know very little about. There are many options out there — just do a search on 'volunteer' and you should find sites that will help you find what you want.

Notes:

_____

_____

_____

_____

_____

_____

_____

Don't have regrets

If you were to live your life as you are currently, would you have any regrets years down the line? It could be not following your most desired career or not visiting a country you've always yearned to see. It could even be not devoting enough time to certain people, or a hobby. Write them down and think about the steps you can take to make those changes. Your next task is to put those steps into action!

Notes:

_____
_____
_____
_____
_____
_____
_____
_____

End procrastination now

This week, finish those tasks that have been on your to-do list for weeks or even months but you have been putting off. So much time is spent avoiding certain tasks, possibly even longer than is spent actually doing the task. Imagine the feeling of accomplishment as you finally finish the task and realise that you never have to face it again.

Notes:

_____

_____

_____

_____

_____

_____

_____

Give a compliment

This week, take the time to give out compliments to other people, without expecting one back. It can be to friends, family, colleagues or complete strangers you happen across during your day. Of course, if you do receive a compliment back, smile and say thank you!

Notes:

_____

_____

_____

_____

_____

_____

_____

_____

Remember your reasons

You have your goal but have yet to achieve it. Try asking yourself the following: "Why did I decide to pursue the goal in the first place? Why is it so important to me?" If you feel yourself struggling with your goal, take some time to think about why you wanted to achieve it. Reconnect with the thoughts and emotions that initially pushed you into action, writing them down to refer to when motivation is low.

Notes:

_____

_____

_____

_____

_____

_____

_____

Focus on your partner

Take the time to compliment your partner. It's so easy to take them for granted or worse, become consumed by their flaws. Instead, try to focus on their good characteristics. As for their faults, try putting a positive spin on them. Remember, you can't change other people but you can change how you think and feel about them.

Notes:

_____

_____

_____

_____

_____

_____

_____

_____

Acts of kindness

Starting today, carry out an act of kindness. Just one. For now. It can be for a friend, stranger, anyone, even an animal. It is up to you what to do and can involve your time or your money, although it does not have to take much of either. Keep an eye out for opportunities to help and then go for it. If you can, make that act anonymous. As you get used to doing them, hopefully you can increase your acts of kindness each day, so eventually they become a part of your life.

Notes:

_____

_____

_____

_____

_____

_____

_____

Eat to increase positive mood

Want something to boost your mood? Forget the junk food. Instead try bananas, avocados, nuts and seeds, all of which have been found to lift your spirits.

Notes:

_____

_____

_____

_____

_____

_____

_____

Imagine you have achieved your goal

When you start to question your ability to achieve your desired goal, sit back and imagine you have already achieved it. Imagine what you feel like, what you are doing, where you are and what other people are saying and doing. Let your imagination run riot. Hopefully this will give you the motivation to reach that goal.

Notes:

_____
_____
_____
_____
_____
_____
_____

Carry out a secret good deed

This week do a good deed for another person. It can be for anyone you know (I wonder how you would feel doing it for someone you did not like very much?). The deed can be anything, large or small; it comes down to your time and imagination. Now here's the twist — keep the good deed secret. Do not tell anyone you did it. If asked if you did it, deny it. This is a very powerful way to increase your happiness.

Notes:

_____

_____

_____

_____

_____

_____

_____

_____

Help others learn

If you delegate work, this tip is for you. If the work comes back not as good as you would like it, don't shy away from delegating or correct the work yourself. Instead use your knowledge to explain what went wrong or needs improvement. Allow the person the chance to learn the right way to do things. Never assume they are not willing to learn or not up to the challenge.

Notes:

_____

_____

_____

_____

_____

_____

_____

Making up

If you have fallen out with someone, be the first to make up. You really will feel better for it. You don't have to say sorry, but if you are, go ahead and say it!

Notes:

_____
_____
_____
_____
_____
_____
_____
_____

Support a cause

Make time to support a cause that is meaningful to you. It is an opportunity to develop your sense of citizenship, as you become part of an organisation with common goals. It is also a chance to express kindness and to learn from others. The extent you get involved is up to you and you can expand on your existing skills or develop new ones.

Notes:

_____
_____
_____
_____
_____
_____
_____
_____

Reward your steps

Each time you take a step closer to your intended goal, give yourself a reward. It can be anything you want it to be, so long as it does not hinder you reaching the goal. Just giving yourself a pat on the back is a great reward.

Notes:

_____

_____

_____

_____

_____

_____

_____

_____

Exercise to increase positive mood

If you're feeling fed up, try exercising. Ten minutes of exercise (after warming up) is all that is needed to decrease negative mood, according to researchers at Northern Arizona University.

Notes:

_____

_____

_____

_____

_____

_____

_____

Five good things

At the end of each day, think of five good things that have happened to you. If you are struggling, even things like getting a seat on the train, or getting to work on time, count. It is a simple way of evaluating your life in a positive light.

Notes:

_____

_____

_____

_____

_____

_____

_____

_____

List your interests

Make a list of your top ten interests. This is your private list so you can be truly honest. You do not have to say those things that you may be expected to say in a job interview. Once you have your list, have a good look at it. Is there anything there which you have neglected or would like to do more of? If so, make a pact with yourself to do something about it.

Notes:

_____

_____

_____

_____

_____

_____

_____

Goodness

This week, try to see the good in everyone. Try not to jump to negative conclusions about a person's behaviour or their possible intentions. Such an activity may help raise awareness of possible prejudices or generalisations you make. It may also help you develop a more balanced perspective — especially if you are the sort of person that makes assumptions about what people are thinking (in particular, about you).

Notes:

_____

_____

_____

_____

_____

_____

_____

Get childish

This week, make time to have fun. What did you enjoy doing as a child? What have you seen children doing that you've wondered what it would be like to do? Then go for it! Be a child for just a little while. There's no rule that says once we are adults we cannot have fun.

Notes:

_____

_____

_____

_____

_____

_____

_____

Happy days

At the end of each day, write down your happiness level out of 10, 1 being very unhappy and 10 being very happy. Then note the activities that you engaged in on that day. Try to include things you started, things you finished, where you went, who you spoke to. After a few days take a look at your happier days and note what things you tended to do on those days. What you now need to do is try to make an effort to do more of the things that make up a good day for you.

Notes:

_____

_____

_____

_____

_____

_____

_____

_____

Get some daylight

Try to make sure you get outdoors at least once a day. By getting natural daylight it will not only help you feel better about yourself, it will also help you sleep.

Notes:

_____

_____

_____

_____

_____

_____

_____

_____

Get curious

It's time to get curious about the world. You don't have to go trekking to far-flung places (unless you want to) to gain an interest in the world around you. Just take a moment to attend to something, anything! It can be a person, an animal, plant life, an object. Give it some thought. What is it doing? How did it get there? Where did it come from? What is it thinking? You get the idea. Get really curious about what is going on for your chosen item of interest; what role does it play in the world and how does it impact on your life?

Notes:

_____

_____

_____

_____

_____

_____

_____

_____

Discover your creative side

This week, have a go at something creative. So you say you cannot draw, sew or paint. Should that stop you giving it a go? If you like you can join a class, or get a book out of the library. Nobody has to judge your efforts (unless you want them to), just get stuck in. Knitting, pottery, woodwork, kite making, jewellery making, embroidery, origami.... and on and on.

Notes:

_____

_____

_____

_____

_____

_____

_____

_____

Your partner's achievements

The next time your partner comes home with good news, be happy for them. Listen to what they have to say and be proud of what they have achieved. Don't get jealous or think about your own life. Focus on your partner 100% and feel empathy for how they are feeling. If you find this difficult, think about how you would want someone to react to your good news.

Notes:

_____

_____

_____

_____

_____

_____

_____

_____

Free up time

Need to be creative? To stand the best chance of being creative, it is no good trying to work under pressure. Rather, you need to schedule in a sufficient amount of time where you are free to focus totally on the task at hand. Make sure this time is also free from interruptions. So shut the door, switch off your phone and let your creative juices flow!

Notes:

_____

_____

_____

_____

_____

_____

_____

Reflect on happiness

This week, take the time to ask yourself, "what does happiness mean to me?" You could begin by defining your own version of happiness. Then, using your definition, reflect on the things you do in your life that bring you closer to happiness. Also think about the things you would like to do more of, to increase your chances of reaching your definition of happiness. Having reflected, get on and do them!

Notes:

_____

_____

_____

_____

_____

_____

_____

Relax into it

To help you get creative, do something that will relax you beforehand. You might like to exercise, do some yoga, deep breathing, read a few pages of a novel; whatever it is you do to relax. By reducing tension and stress, you will put yourself into a positive frame of mind. This will enable you to set to work on your creative tasks.

Notes:

_____
_____
_____
_____
_____
_____
_____

Express an opinion

Sometimes we are faced with the difficult decision of whether to speak out about something that concerns us, knowing that it risks being unpopular, or to stay quiet and keep the peace. This is especially true if you know your opinion is in the minority. However, having the courage to express your opinion in the face of potential opposition shows you are willing to stand up for what you believe in. You will probably like yourself more than if you had decided to keep quiet.

Notes:

_____
_____
_____
_____
_____
_____
_____
_____

Stories of courage

Spend time collecting stories of people displaying acts of bravery. Consider the following sources: television shows, the news, the internet, newspapers (national and local), things you see in your everyday life, as well as stories people share with you. Let such stories help you define what it means to be brave, and use them to inspire you to be braver in your own life.

Notes:

_____

_____

_____

_____

_____

_____

_____

_____

Be honest

This week take time to be honest with your thoughts and feelings. Don't just say you're fine when you are really fed up or say yes to a task which you really don't want to do. Being honest isn't about being rude to other people; it is about being true to yourself.

Notes:

_____

_____

_____

_____

_____

_____

_____

_____

Take time out

This week, try to find time to get as far away from reality as possible. If you live in the city, go visit the country, or vice versa. Do something that gives you an opportunity to break from routine. Sit in a different chair, drink from a different cup, read a new magazine, go to work at a different time. Do whatever you feel comfortable with, just be sure to give it a go and enjoy it!

Notes:

_____

_____

_____

_____

_____

_____

_____

Rearrange your furniture

This week, how about moving your furniture around a bit? It's a small change that's easily achieved. You may love or hate your new look, but at least you gave it a go. It may even inspire you to change other aspects of your life.

Notes:

_____
_____
_____
_____
_____
_____
_____
_____

Flowers

This week, buy yourself some fresh flowers and display them around your house. Flowers will cheer up your environment and if you change them each week, add variety to your life. It has also been suggested by Dr Alan Hirsch that having flowers in the house can reduce anxiety by 20%.

Notes:

_____

_____

_____

_____

_____

_____

_____

Enhance your senses

Try to pay attention to the world around you, making use of all your senses. It's so easy to ignore the everyday as you've got used to it and so much attention is given to simply what you see. Instead, make a conscious effort to attend to what you feel, hear, taste and smell. In addition, reflect on how what you see today differs to how you saw it originally. For example, your office seems so much smaller now, but when you first walked in it seemed huge and daunting.

Notes:

_____

_____

_____

_____

_____

_____

_____

_____

List of achievements

So often we keep lists of things to do. Some of these get done, some are ignored and some are carried over for another day. However, how about starting a list of achievements? As you see yourself achieving things (no matter how small), keep a note. Not only is this an incentive to get through your things to do list, it will also provide you with an indication of how productive your days actually are.

Notes:

_____

_____

_____

_____

_____

_____

_____

Find beauty and savour it

There is beauty everywhere. Beauty is about all those things that bring you sensory pleasure. This week, make a conscious effort to note the beautiful things in your world. Attend to all that you see, hear, taste, touch and even smell. Try to do this on a daily basis and relish the good feelings evoked through your renewed awareness.

Notes:

_____

_____

_____

_____

_____

_____

_____

_____

What are you proud of?

Think about all the things in your life that you are proud of. What things have you done in your past that you can look back on today and say, "yep, I'm really proud of the way I did that". What about the things you are doing now that you are proud of? As you take the time to reflect on this activity, have a think about what these things tell you about the sort of person you are. You may come to understand a bit more about the things you value and what matters in your life.

Notes:

_____

_____

_____

_____

_____

_____

_____

Write a gratitude letter

There is good evidence that gratitude boosts happiness. An effective means of showing your gratitude is to write a letter to someone who has made a positive difference to your life. This is your opportunity to thank them and let them know the impact they made on you. Send the letter if you can, or even better, read it to them.

Notes:

_____

_____

_____

_____

_____

_____

_____

_____

Savour your email reading

Whenever an email from a friend arrives in your inbox, don't read it straight away. Instead, set aside a particular time to read it, when you are free from any distractions. This way you can focus totally on the email, rather than just glancing through it. Savour the words and enjoy the experience.

Notes:

_____

_____

_____

_____

_____

_____

_____

Resolve conflict quickly

Try to make up as soon as possible after an argument with a friend, spouse, work colleague, or whoever. Doing so frees you from the anger and resentment which could last years if things are not managed well. If you feel it is appropriate, also apologise. It is not a sign of weakness and you will feel better for it.

Notes:

_____

_____

_____

_____

_____

_____

_____

_____

Enjoy the journey

When working on your goals, try to enjoy the journey along the way. Actually achieving the goal will make you feel great, for a while. However, it will not last. So when working on your goals, make sure to enjoy the here and now and learn from the experience.

Notes:

_____

_____

_____

_____

_____

_____

_____

Try something new

Want to learn more about yourself as well as the world around you? Then give something new a go. It doesn't have to be big — maybe a different flavour of cordial instead of what you usually drink. Or it could be a whole new experience — perhaps getting hold of a bike and cycling to work.

Notes:

_____

_____

_____

_____

_____

_____

_____

_____

Look to your past

In facing challenges now and in the future, it can be a good move to look to your past. How have you succeeded previously? What actions did you take to guarantee success? Did you receive support in any way? How can the past inspire you to ensure you meet your goals, and overcome potential setbacks?

Notes:

_____

_____

_____

_____

_____

_____

_____

Question your negative thinking

Learn to recognise negative or unrealistic thoughts when they arise. These include thoughts such as 'I can't', 'never', 'must'. Also note when you underestimate the role you play in something, saying things like 'oh, I was just lucky'. Being aware of such thoughts means you can go on and challenge them and replace them with more realistic ones. Thoughts influence our actions.

Notes:

_____

_____

_____

_____

_____

_____

_____

_____

Get support

If you are working on goals, whether large or small, try to obtain support from others. Choose people who you know will encourage and inspire you and help renew your energies when things start to dwindle. If you run into difficulties, consult them for ideas to help you figure out and implement potential solutions.

Notes:

_____

_____

_____

_____

_____

_____

_____

Go outside

Try to spend at least some time outdoors each week. Preferably not spent walking up and down the shopping mall. Rather, you could go for a walk or a run, get on a bike, or perhaps get more adventurous and plan a hike. Take in your surroundings; get energised and inspired.

Notes:

_____
_____
_____
_____
_____
_____
_____
_____

Try not to multitask

When you are multitasking, your attention is compromised. Try to become aware of when you multitask, and make an effort to just focus on one task at a time. As such, the task will get your undivided attention and chances are you will do even better at it. It also increases your chance of experiencing flow which is a great way to experience happiness.

Notes:

_____

_____

_____

_____

_____

_____

_____

Reduce your distractions

If you find yourself procrastinating, make a deliberate effort to limit your distractions. Can you switch your phone off, close down your computer, turn off the TV? Note what is getting in the way of you achieving the thing you are aiming for and make the necessary changes. Because procrastination is a drain on your time.

Notes:

_____

_____

_____

_____

_____

_____

_____

_____

Review your work / life balance

Are you suffering from stress, spending far more time working than at leisure? Each day, try recording how many hours are spent working and how many at leisure. Then take gradual steps to balance this out, allowing yourself extra time each day for leisure activities. Note how you spend your leisure time, to ensure you make the most of it.

Notes:

_____

_____

_____

_____

_____

_____

_____

Enjoy every day

Take the time to reflect on every day of the week and consider the benefits of each. What do you enjoy doing and what do you look forward to that happens on that day in particular? If there is one day where the list is short, what can you do to increase the good points?

Notes:

_____
_____
_____
_____
_____
_____
_____
_____

Peter meet Peter

If you met yourself, would you like you? Give this some thought and try to be honest. Are there any habits, behaviours or characteristics that you have which you know you would find irritating if you had to spend time with you? What changes could you make so that you and yourself can happily spend time on a desert island together?

Notes:

_____

_____

_____

_____

_____

_____

_____

Be more curious

An easy way to enhance your curiosity is to learn more about something that already interests you. Think about your favourite hobby. What is there that you still know little about or have yet to try? As you attempt to find out these answers, your curiosity hopefully will increase your enthusiasm for something you already enjoy and of course, your happiness.

Notes:

_____
_____
_____
_____
_____
_____
_____
_____

Past, present, future

How do you see yourself in time? Do you tend to look to your past, spending time reminiscing? Or do you focus on the present, neither looking to your past or your future. Or are you concerned solely with the future? Ideally, strive for a balance between all three: looking fondly to your past, enjoying your present and being hopeful about the future.

Notes:

_____

_____

_____

_____

_____

_____

_____

Other people

Take the time to appreciate the qualities of others. It's very easy to think highly of those characteristics that we ourselves possess and we go on to evaluate other people accordingly. So if you can, take a moment to observe someone you easily criticise and notice the good things they offer and the strengths they display.

Notes:

_____
_____
_____
_____
_____
_____
_____
_____

Watch Harold and Maud

Have you seen the movie Harold and Maud? If not, hire it this weekend. If you have, watch it again. If there's one movie that can inspire us to get the most out of life, then this has to be it. Learn from what you see and then promise yourself you will act on what you have learned.

Notes:

_____

_____

_____

_____

_____

_____

_____

Boost your vitality

Having a real zest for life has been highly correlated with happiness. So make sure you have sufficient resources to ensure you have enough energy and enthusiasm to make the most of your day. Eat well (don't forget about breakfast and lay off the junk food), get enough sleep and make time to exercise.

Notes:

_____

_____

_____

_____

_____

_____

_____

_____

Have a banana

What you eat can have an impact on how happy you feel. If you want to increase your mood, go for foods that contain tryptophan, since they raise your serotonin levels. With increased serotonin, you may end up feeling more resilient, comfortable, safer and happier. Bananas do just that, as well as nuts and oats.

Notes:

_____
_____
_____
_____
_____
_____
_____

Keep it personal

As you read all the tips, ideas and research findings that promote ways to increase your happiness, try to think how it will work for you personally. Circumstances can be a factor, but also consider your personality, strengths and goals in deciding ways you are going to increase your happiness. Adapt what you read about happiness to suit you.

Notes:

_____

_____

_____

_____

_____

_____

_____

_____

Mix things up

Participating in a variety of activities may be the key to happiness. So as you continue on your happiness journey, bear in mind that doing the same thing over and over means it may become stale. Try to monitor how you feel about a particular activity to check it is still adding to, rather than taking away from your happiness.

Notes:

_____

_____

_____

_____

_____

_____

_____

Get excited

When you next make plans, commit yourself to the task with energy and determination. Whether it is planning something to do at the weekend, your next holiday or an evening out, really get involved and be enthusiastic. Don't assume things will go wrong and if you can, involve people who will match or even surpass your energy.

Notes:

_____

_____

_____

_____

_____

_____

_____

_____

Share your learning

Try sharing with others the knowledge you have acquired about what makes a happier life. Hopefully the recipient will learn something which inspires them to make positive changes in their life. Sharing this happiness stuff may also help keep you on the track of your own happiness path and keep you inspired and uplifted.

Notes:

_____

_____

_____

_____

_____

_____

_____

Check the details

When working on a project, take the time to check that all the relevant details have been covered. Keep lists if necessary. Not only will you feel more in control throughout the project, you are also less likely to have that stomach-churning experience when you realise you'd forgotten a particular detail, but it's too late to change it.

Notes:

_____

_____

_____

_____

_____

_____

_____

_____

Bedside cabinet

Take a look at the contents of your bedside cabinet. Is there anything special there that brings you joy or pleasure? If not, take the time to place things on it that do just that. It's one of the last things you see before you go to sleep each night, so you may as well have things on it that you enjoy.

Notes:

_____

_____

_____

_____

_____

_____

_____

Displays of loyalty

Try to be loyal to your friends and family and support them as needed. Sometimes this is about putting their needs before your own. People want to be supported and your loyal actions will be appreciated. It may help to recall times when people have displayed their loyalty towards you. Remember how it felt to have someone in your corner?

Notes:

_____

_____

_____

_____

_____

_____

_____

_____

Forget the rules

I must do this, I should do that. We have these rules that can sometimes dominate our life. It's your life and so the rules you live by should be your own. For instance, decorate your house how you want it to be and do not worry about whether your visitors will 'approve'. Or read the books you want, rather than the ones you feel you ought.

Notes:

_____

_____

_____

_____

_____

_____

_____

Rate your work

How did you do on your last project (whether home or work related)? Did you give it your all? Was the work to your highest quality? Did you achieve perfection, or can you see where you could have made improvements? Take the time to evaluate your own work and use what you learned for your next project.

Notes:

_____

_____

_____

_____

_____

_____

_____

_____

Vary your routine

Feeling stuck in a rut? If you suddenly realise your routine is the same day in, day out, try mixing things up a bit. It only has to be a few small changes (or even one small change) to make a difference to how you feel about your day. For example, vary your morning routine, eat something different or start work earlier (or later).

Notes:

_____

_____

_____

_____

_____

_____

_____

Imagine it – then do it

Struggling with a goal, lacking the necessary motivation to see you through to the end? Then try some imagery. Close your eyes and imagine yourself performing the task. Bring to life how good it feels to be working on your goal. Keep going until you really feel energised. Then go do it!

Notes:

_____
_____
_____
_____
_____
_____
_____

Time to celebrate

Each day or week, find a reason to celebrate. It will break up the routine of your day or week. What was good for you? What did you achieve or what went particularly well? So how will you celebrate? With friends? Family? Or alone, spending time doing something you love? It could be something as simple as relaxing in front of the TV.

Notes:

_____

_____

_____

_____

_____

_____

_____

Gratitude emails

When doing catch-up emails to friends and family reflect on the good things in your life as well as the people who supported you through a trying time and let this be the focus of your email. It'll give you a boost as you realise the good in your life and will hopefully lift your reader also.

Notes:

_____

_____

_____

_____

_____

_____

_____

_____

Tune into your body

Spend time trying to understand what your body is saying to you. How is it feeling right now? Work your way down your body — is there any discomfort? Do this exercise throughout the day, as you eat, drink, work and exercise. Increasing your awareness may help you make better choices in what you put in — and how you treat — your body.

Notes:

_____

_____

_____

_____

_____

_____

_____

Set yourself a challenge

Have you challenged yourself lately? Whether it is a mental or physical, setting then going for a challenge can be very energising. You have something new to focus on, that engages you for the duration of the challenge. Set a deadline for your challenge and make sure to schedule time for it so you don't let it drift.

Notes:

_____

_____

_____

_____

_____

_____

_____

_____

The perfect image

Imagine the perfect you. I mean this in terms of personal characteristics and attributes, rather than physical aspects. What sort of person would you be? How would you relate to others, respond to difficulties, go about your everyday life? Now how close are you to this perfect image? Are there any steps you can take to become the perfect you?

Notes:

_____
_____
_____
_____
_____
_____
_____
_____

Choose your quote

For any topic, viewpoint or feeling, there is probably a quotation that sums it up. Do you have a favourite quote that speaks personally to you? If not, seek yours out and use those words to remind you of what you want to become, or how you want to live your life. Feeling creative? Compose your own.

Notes:

_____

_____

_____

_____

_____

_____

_____

_____

Answerphone message

Small changes can help break up your routine and give you a lift. So how about making a new message for your phone/s? Whether it is your home phone, mobile or work phone, try to inject a bit of you in the message. Of course, be mindful of the recipient, but there's no reason why you can't have fun.

Notes:

_____

_____

_____

_____

_____

_____

_____

Share happy news

News sites are generally full of all that is awful in the world (although you may want to look at HappyNews.com). From reading them, you can end up feeling powerless and despondent. So when you read news that is uplifting and cheery, share it with people who you know will appreciate a mood boost.

Notes:

_____

_____

_____

_____

_____

_____

_____

_____

Forgive sooner

Rather than letting quarrels continue on for hours, days, or even longer (sometimes years), make a decision to make up, forgive and move on quickly. Not only will your relationships be better, but you will feel better yourself, as you are able to focus on more important things.

Notes:

_____
_____
_____
_____
_____
_____
_____

The week ahead

Think about the next seven days. What are you looking forward to on each day? Ideally, think of something different for each day, therefore making each day distinct from the others. From doing this exercise, hopefully you will realise how much you have to look forward to — whether the day is Tuesday or Saturday.

Notes:

_____

_____

_____

_____

_____

_____

_____

_____

Regrets

Having regrets can mean a life of misery. You feel irritated and helpless. If only I had done x. Yet the reality is, what's done is done and you cannot change the past. So try and spend time thinking about the reasons why it is not worth having regrets. Maybe do some research to discover the impact it can have on your wellbeing. Once you understand that holding on to regrets isn't healthy, perhaps you can finally overcome yours?

Notes:

_____

_____

_____

_____

_____

_____

_____

Ignore negative people

If you worry too much about what people think, you can find yourself stuck, going nowhere fast. Even worse is when the people you are worrying about are full of criticism and scepticism for your plans and ideas. Remember that people can be uneasy with change and may try to hold back people trying to get ahead, in an attempt to maintain their own comfort levels.

Notes:

_____

_____

_____

_____

_____

_____

_____

_____

Achievements

Have you reflected on your achievements lately? Both large and small. Begin by reflecting back over your life on the significant things you have done. From there, continue to build on your list, by making a note each month of the things you have achieved. Even better, add to it as they happen. This way you don't forget and will realise how much you do accomplish.

Notes:

_____

_____

_____

_____

_____

_____

_____

Doing what you love

Are you doing what you love? At least some of the time? There's ample opportunity each and every day to be doing things we dislike, find mundane or irritating. Yet if you make the effort to find time to do the things you enjoy on a weekly basis then you will cope with the mundane much more easily. An even better plan would be to look for pleasure in the things you dislike.

Notes:

_____

_____

_____

_____

_____

_____

_____

_____

Top memories

Thinking back over the past twelve months, what are your top five memories? What were you doing? Who were you with? What makes that moment so special? Based on what you learnt, what do you need to do to ensure more good memories? Struggling to think of five? Then make changes to your life to ensure, in twelve months' time you will be spoilt for choice.

Notes:

_____

_____

_____

_____

_____

_____

_____

Sharing your goals

If you have a large goal that you want to achieve, don't keep it to yourself. Choose a select number of people and let them know your plans. Now you have said your goal out loud, you have to get on and do it right? Offer them regular updates on your progress and use their support for motivation.

Notes:

_____

_____

_____

_____

_____

_____

_____

Give them a smile

Stop reading this a sec, turn to face someone, then give them a smile. Brighten your day, brighten their day. All alone? Then get up and go find someone to smile at. If you still can't find anyone and don't fancy wandering the streets then just go find a mirror and give yourself a smile. That wasn't so bad now was it?

Notes:

_____

_____

_____

_____

_____

_____

_____

_____

Get better sleep

Set your alarm then turn your clock so it is facing the wall and you can no longer see it. This way you are no longer worrying about what the time is and how many hours before you have to get up. After all, this time is scheduled for sleep, so it really doesn't matter what the time is.

Notes:

_____

_____

_____

_____

_____

_____

_____

_____

Do something creative

Ever had a novel idea? Perhaps a different way of doing things? Or you finally have a solution to an ongoing problem. Your idea doesn't have to be huge to make an impact. Now you have your creative idea, make sure you do something with it. Don't dismiss it — it could be something great. What's the worst that could happen?

Notes:

_____
_____
_____
_____
_____
_____
_____

A good day

Do you struggle for time, wondering where it's gone with very little achieved? An activity that might help is to write a description of a day where your time is well spent. What are you doing? What distractions are you avoiding? Now what steps can you take to bring your well spent day in alignment with your actual day to day routine?

Notes:

_____

_____

_____

_____

_____

_____

_____

_____

Prove yourself to yourself

Prove that you can change. That you are stronger than you ever thought possible. Give up a habit for a week, or even a month. It does not have to be one of your worst habits — but enough to be a learning experience. From there, you may want to build on your success and break the habit for good, or choose something you know will be life altering.

Notes:

_____

_____

_____

_____

_____

_____

_____

Varied goals

Do your goals tend to be around specific areas? Perhaps you focus more on career, but neglect your emotional wellbeing. Take the time to consider different areas of your life and set yourself achievable goals for each. Areas you might want to include are: career goals, financial goals, personal growth, education, leisure, family, relationship goals, health, spiritual and social.

Notes:

_____

_____

_____

_____

_____

_____

_____

No more poor me

If you have the courage to take responsibility for your life and all that happens in it, you are freeing yourself up to have a fantastic life. No longer at the mercy of other people's decisions, or blaming others when things go wrong. Instead you will stop feeling like a victim with no control and become someone who is genuinely living their own life. What can be better than that?

Notes:

_____

_____

_____

_____

_____

_____

_____

_____

What will you stop doing?

If you want to make time for a particular project or activity, then you will need to make an important decision. What are you going to stop doing? Because you are always doing something (even staring at the walls is something, it's just not that productive). So you must decide what you are going to do less of, or give up altogether, in order to make time for your new plans.

Notes:

_____

_____

_____

_____

_____

_____

_____

_____

The weekend

Do something different at the weekend. Feel free to plan ahead, but a break from routine can be very revitalising. Also, it gets you out of a rut, will help get you excited about life and will give your brain a workout. You are no longer following the same pattern, so will have to think about your actions.

Notes:

_____

_____

_____

_____

_____

_____

_____

Happy relationships

Give your relationship a happiness boost with some easy to implement ideas. Give your partner a hug on a daily basis. Whilst there, say something nice. Show them you are grateful they are in your life. When you can, hold their hand. Finally, remember to talk to them — don't let issues build up. This also means resolving conflicts sooner rather than later.

Notes:

_____

_____

_____

_____

_____

_____

_____

_____

Don't disappoint

Try to keep the promises and agreements you've made with another. Whether it is keeping a time to meet a friend for lunch, or meeting a request to do a particular task, try to follow through. Even better, put the effort in to do something ahead of time, or arrive early for an appointment. You'll feel good and so will the other person.

Notes:

_____
_____
_____
_____
_____
_____
_____

And finally

For health and happiness, try these three things. First, learn how to cook. Cooking all you eat makes you aware of what you are putting into your body. Second, exercise. Workouts are good for body and mind, so make them part of your life. Finally, cut down on your television watching habit, giving you time to do all those things you want to do.

Notes:

_____

_____

_____

_____

_____

_____

_____

_____